HOW TO GET YOUR EX BACK

THE RULE GUIDE TO FIX YOUR RELATIONSHIP BREAKUP
FAST AND GET YOUR MAN TO LOVE YOU AGAIN

Descrierea CIP a Bibliotecii Naționale a României
GOTTMAN, MARY
　How to get your ex back : the rule guide to fix your relationship breakup fast and get your man to love you again / by Mary Gottman. - București : My Ebook, 2018
　ISBN 978-606-983-613-2

159.9

HOW TO GET YOUR EX BACK

THE RULE GUIDE TO FIX YOUR RELATIONSHIP BREAKUP FAST AND GET YOUR MAN TO LOVE YOU AGAIN

My Ebook Publishing House
Bucharest, 2018

CONTENTS

Chapter 1. GOOD RELATIONSHIPS ARE SWEET 13
Chapter 2. BIOLOGICAL DIFFERENCE 18
Chapter 3. SOME OTHER REASONS FOR
                 CONFLICTS IN RELATIONSHIPS 25
Chapter 4. SOME POSSIBLE MISTAKES 33
Chapter 5. PREVENTING FAIRY TALE
                 EXPERIENCES 39
Chapter 6. DON'T AGREE ALL AT ONCE:
                 BE HARD TO GET 44
Conclusion 51

INTRODUCTION

I want to thank you and congratulate you for purchasing this book, *"How To Get Your Ex Back: The Rule Guide To Fix Your Relationship Breakup Fast And Get Your Man To Love You Again."* This book contains proven steps and strategies on *How to get your ex back*. It also gives an insight into the activities of how to deal with your ex, so you don't look desperate.

Thanks again for buying this book, I hope you enjoy it!

Copyright 2018 by Zen Mastery - All rights reserved

This document is geared towards providing exact and reliable information in regards to the topic and issue covered. The publication is sold with the idea that the publisher is not required to render accounting, officially permitted, or otherwise, qualified services. If advice is necessary, legal or professional, a practiced individual in the profession should be ordered.

- From a Declaration of Principles which was accepted and approved equally by a Committee of the American Bar Association and a Committee of Publishers and Associations.

In no way is it legal to reproduce, duplicate, or transmit any part of this document in either electronic means or in printed format. Recording of this publication is strictly prohibited and any storage of this document is not allowed unless with written permission from the publisher. All rights reserved.

The information provided herein is stated to be truthful and consistent, in that any liability, in terms of inattention or otherwise, by any usage or abuse of any policies, processes, or directions contained within is the solitary and utter responsibility of the recipient reader. Under no circumstances will any legal responsibility or blame be held against the publisher for any reparation, damages, or monetary loss due to the information herein, either directly or indirectly.

Respective authors own all copyrights not held by the publisher.

The information herein is offered for informational purposes solely, and is universal as so. The presentation of the information is without contract or any type of guarantee assurance.

The trademarks that are used are without any consent, and the publication of the trademark is without permission or backing by the trademark owner. All trademarks and brands within this book are for clarifying purposes only and are the owned by the owners themselves, not affiliated with this document.

CHAPTER ONE
GOOD RELATIONSHIPS ARE SWEET

To be in a good relationship is one of the best things that can happen to anyone, this is so because there is a constant flow of bliss that goes around anyone that is in a joyful relationship. Relationships can help you become focused and create a life that would surpass all others that you have lived. But sometimes, the good relationship fails. The very best relationship can go sour, and it is a very sad happening. When this happens, there is bitterness and sour feeling. No matter what happens in a relationship, there is a reason for it. There is nothing that just happens from the blue. Life is about cause and effects and not just probability.

There are several reasons why many relationships go to the winds and park up. It can be from a range of character adjustment or manipulations; which can lead to distrust and hate among persons in relationship. Reasons may include; reduced communications. It may also be caused by incessant arguments and quarrels.

Several persons bother about the whereabouts of their partners, and they seem hurt and unsure of how and where their partners are; this action by them is not the smartest, rather it is the opposite of what they should be doing at the instance.

Firstly, it is very important to note that men and women think differently hence they should have a different reaction and action line. Men will like to do the things that would sound rational to them while women will not leave their way to act the way men do, rather they will behave classically as women behave.

Using the logic of a male to try to win your love back is a very wrong approach and will not yield any efforts. It will be so unwise and irrational to expect a lady to think just as men do and vice versa. The men should not expect the women to think like them; hence any approach towards the female folks should be geared towards reacting as they do.

The painful reality is that both parties may be sincerely in love with themselves, but they will not know exactly what actions are really pushing the other away. Intentions may be very good, but the fact remains, if laws and principles of a relationship are not followed, then it will be difficult to unite the male and female in a relationship.

This implies that some are completely doing the opposite actions that will not bring a positive result in bringing back your former lover. Think about your actions so far, is what you are currently doing helping you to win back your lover or is it just driving them away from you and even making you feel worse than you used to.

We are going to check some of the basic things that men and women think differently about in a relationship, no matter the intentions behind them. They view the actions of their partners so differently and just like has been previously stated, intentions only matter to you and not your partner. It would be outrightly useless if your intentions are not appropriately communicated.

These basic things we are about to analyze will cause a great revolution in your step in winning back your ex. It will help you know what really went wrong before and how you can amend it to get something fruitful from it.

CHAPTER TWO
BIOLOGICAL DIFFERENCE

There is, at least, a remarkable biological difference between the male and the female. However, many may think this is stating the obvious, but it isn't. This point is stated to let us understand that there are some very vital hormonal differences and other differences associated with moods in the females, that may be absent in the males.

A very good illustration of this hormonal difference is the fact that males sometimes and frequently will want to increase their testosterone levels when they are stressed just to increase their ability to relax and overcome the ensuing stress that results. This means that the news would not make them relax as much as undergoing some romance, or light sex. That is how the body of the male is configured.

When these testosterone levels are increased, the male will feel happier and better about themselves. And only then they can feel like helping the world and solve other issues that are not close to their immediate needs that relate to their shelter and food. However, unfortunately, women are not wired in such manner. Women have opposite emotional drives. And if this is not handled properly, it can be a major cause of conflict in a relationship. When a woman stress level is increased, she would want to solve them outright; directly proferring solutions to every of the difficulty and not using any emotional exercise to calm things down.

When a female gets back from the office, she is stressed after a hectic day; her body is wired to do the necessary chores and sleep, only this way she can be rejuvenated for the next day's activities. But, just as I have explained above, it is not so for the male partner; he needs and uses other means to relax his body and get focused.

Hence for a typical situation when the female is not in the mood to satisfy the activities of the male, then without rational thought line, there can be a little quarrel, and that can lead to major conflict and hamper relationships.

In some case, in order to reduce stress, the women will try to secret the female hormone known as Oxytocin. This hormone stimulates the feminine nature of the female and helps them develop into having characteristic feminine behavior. But for women to produce this hormone, they need to feel loved and catered for. They need to feel highly appreciated. But when they don't feel this way, that is, when they feel their partner not showing them the necessary attention and love, the secretion of this female hormone is drastically reduced. And this increases their stress level.

Also, a man stress level will increase if he doesn't find a way of increasing his testosterone levels. This is greatly interesting stuff, right?

Now, for some relationship, you realized that this misunderstanding is what led to the conflict before. Well, now you know, this will already give you the ability to resolve that conflict and understand better your partner to achieve a blissful result.

Hormones Can Destroy Blissful Relationships

Just try to remember some of the times when you have been in a perfect mood waiting for your partner to arrive. As a lady, you may have done some activities to raise your oxytocin level; you may have spoken to your friends and feel very relaxed. There are many other activities that can raise your oxytocin levels and maybe you have done all those, on purpose or just unknowingly. But when your ex returned from work, all he wants to do is freshen up and undergo some activities that would reduce his stress level. He doesn't want to talk to anyone. If he talks and spends any more time doing something else, his stress level will spike further. But instead, he comes home to meet a partner who wants to talk and share all her thoughts with him; a partner that is expecting him to listen to all her thought line (the females usually do the thinking and run them through their partners) and when he is not ready for this? A conflict ensues.

He has not had the time to remove the stress of the day from his body, yet he is faced with a partner who is relaxed and does not seem to understand his needs at all. This is a typical example, but you have to notice that even the most joyous relationships will be destroyed by misunderstanding this hormonal imbalance.

Of course, I do not mean that there are not other causes of misunderstanding in a relationship. There are, a lot more other reasons for breakups and other conflicts but the conflicts caused by hormones are much more subtle and difficult to notice if the hormonal characteristics of the partner are not well understood.

CHAPTER THREE
SOME OTHER REASONS FOR CONFLICTS IN RELATIONSHIPS

There are some other instances where you have tried your best to keep things together between you and your partner but your ex still doesn't feel the energy within but rather still shows signs of boredom and lack of interest in the relationship.

There are sometimes when you think everything is doing fine and going nice but then suddenly, your ex just stops returning calls and messages. They may just end all communication channels without any further reasons as to why they made the decision. Yes! It can be that bad.

And whenever the discussion is brought to bear, the shunned partner always play the innocent card, they seem as if they have done nothing wrong and all of the faults belong to the other partner who left them in the lurch. Actually, the partner who gradually withdrew from the relationship may not have been satisfied with the direction the relationship was going after all.

Okay, here is the fact, when people fall in love, there is a particular hormone that they emit. This hormone is very similar to the ones secreted when persons suffer from a disease called the Obsessive Compulsive Disorder OCD. This explains the reason why persons who are in love can't really think of any other one around them except the person that they are in a relationship with. They can't eat, sleep properly and cannot even concentrate at work.

And the fact remains that, because you are feeling this way doesn't mean that your partner will feel this same way too. Maybe yes, also, maybe they will feel the same way, but just some other time. This illustration explains it; not everyone gets hungry the same time. Hence not everyone will feel the cheese about the relationship together with their partners, although some do.

However, here is the unfortunate part of the whole scenario; one person in the relationship may be the one working for the progress of the relationship. They may be the one trying to fix the relationship in perfect shape and helping next partner see what is positive about the relationship.

This thought line can lead to a person thinking that the relationship has progressed into something else. This can be so for a while as the other person is still in the process of checking out the relationship and knowing what is best for them.

This can seem frustrating. While one partner seems to be just dating, the other one is in a full-time relationship and expecting the other partner to reciprocate the efforts. The biggest mistake here can be when the overly excited partner would begin to look for means to express to the other how much they love them or how urgent they need the relationship to improve and go to the next stage. This act alone can be counter-productive. When men notice this kind of behavior in women, it makes them want to end the relationship or just slow things further; and does not turn them on, it reduces their interest.

When a woman is desperate and insecure; it turns men off!

However, this does not really apply same to the male; they can go any length in expressing their love and affection for ladies. They would make the lady feel on top of the world. The main problem with this case is that they are really ignorant of the consequences of their actions; it will ruin the relationship in the long run.

The Beginning has the Answers

Every of the story of love always has a fantastic beginning. Even for the worse relationship, there was a time when the partners would be overly excited about them and be so nice to each other. Hence in almost every cases of break up, the points needed to get your ex back lies at the beginning of the relationship.

What was the thrill about your partner when you first met them? What did you like about them initially? Where you guys altogether happy?

There is a high chance that the both of you were happy and lived in your best behavior. You both ensured that there was happiness and joy amongst yourselves. You both overlooked the other person's behavior and tried to be nice irrespective of the opposing condition. Now, try to check the last time you spent with your ex, was there any excitement in your midst? Did you enjoy each other's companionship? Was there stress in the air, or were you guys worried about what the other person was thinking?

And if you guys were not getting on perfectly, it seems that the image your ex has of you is that of an aggressive, arguing, upset and worried partner. This kind of thought is not the best kind of thought a partner should have of his ex. Usually, when a relationship ends, the separated partners are looking for someone who would fit into the position of their ex when they first met them.

Yes, the person you were when you guys met is the stellar character that your partner needs to keep seeing in order to kindle that love. It must have been motivating, happy, confident and independent personality. There would be a fire that they needed to see when they first met you.

What changed?

The next thing to talk about is to analyze the mistakes you have made and then how to go about them.

CHAPTER FOUR
SOME POSSIBLE MISTAKES

There are some mistakes many partners make in trying to get their ex back. They seem desperate, and because of the panic of losing the partners, they tend to use all means possible to get them back. Some try to convince their partner of the fact that they need to be together with them for the rest of their lives. But it usually doesn't work out as the ex does not feel the same way.

If you tried calling or texting your ex and doing al best to convince them that you are the perfect person for their life; there is a high chance that you are driving them further away from you and you may not achieve in the long run the intentions you had in mind. The main problem with this comeback acts is that your ex is not seeing them as a romantic turn but rather as desperation on your part. The habit is just an expression of insecurity, and it is not a trait you want to be identified with you in a relationship. No one likes clinginess, and it turns your partner off; learn to give breathing space.

A partner who is confident is what is needed; everyone likes a confident person in a relationship. It creates attractiveness in a relationship and helps to build trust. Anyone who knows exactly what he wants and does not depend on someone else to get it done is surely confident, and that nature is attractive.

However, anyone who becomes unsure about themselves and the suddenly becomes attached to their partner in every way becomes unattractive. Just reflect on your past and understand that your partner had fallen in love with a confident, bubbling and attractive personality. And then when you display the miserable and desperate nature, you send your partner further away from reaching out to you and being passionate about you.

No one would be happy spending time with anyone who begs, plead, argues and making attempts at convincing them at doing something. In fact, when someone tries to convince you to do something for too long, you avoid their presence and ignore their efforts to reach you. Except the

If you have already fallen a victim of being so desperate to get your ex back, do not worry, there are some ways to overcome and reset your impressions to be perfect again. If you have been guilty of sending constant emails and calls, then you may have sent them further away from you instead of closer. The next chapter will deal on how to reverse this mistake.

Reversing Past Errors

This chapter will deal the best point in this book you should never forget in a hurry. The first step in winning your ex back is to avoid contacting your ex in any way. Never make the mistake in any way. This is irrespective of the need to have them back. As you have seen in previous chapters, desperation drives your ex further away from you. Stop calling, texting. Do not ask about them from friends - just stop!

This is the next thing to do; think about who you used to be before you met them, you were getting along just fine and did not have any problems. You had something that occupied your thoughts before your ex came on board. Go back to them. Connect with your old friends, hang out. Resume your job and just be your normal you again. This process may take days to fit-in but then never be too anxious. Take the necessary steps as I have explained, this will help you get across properly.

You may not feel like this, but try to engage yourself to prevent your sad emotions from putting you in a difficult condition; don't sit at home waiting for the phone to ring. Try to engage yourself and put a smile on your face; this will make you feel good and cheerful.

In this period, try to avoid people who are negative in thinking. Some friends may want to make you feel bad about losing your lost love and then put in you a sad appearance. This will help you recover fast and return back the cheerful and happy person your ex met before falling in love in the first place. Once you do this, your ex will begin to care about you and worry. Although they may not express this to you but trust me, they will be on the lookout for your calls and texts.

Finally, the important lesson is for you not to call your ex, rather what you have to do is work on yourself and try to control what is happening in yourself.

CHAPTER FIVE
PREVENTING FAIRY TALE EXPERIENCES

Several factors affect our relationship, and the way we relate to them will affect ourselves through the decisions that we make. But among all these factors, the movie industry, that is the Hollywood movies. These movies have made us think that after we have had issues with our relationships, suddenly there would be a dramatic switch and we will live ever happy with our spouse after they return to their senses; just like that!

That is a fairy tale, and we should not live like that. In fact, nothing ever happens just as they portray in the movies! The real truth is that your ex doesn't play any role in you being happy. Happiness is a choice. The earlier you understand this, the better for you. Never place your happiness on anyone. You just need to be yourself and be your best self; being yourself, and on purpose, will make you happy and give you the different desires that you looked for in your partners.

Try to remember; when you first met your ex, you were very passionate, independent and confident. Chances are, these are the qualities that got your ex attracted to you. So try to loosen up and have some fun. Return to that your cheerful self once again. Try hanging out with some friends, catch some cinema movies, get a new haircut; just spend the time to look and feel good.

When you feel good about yourself, then you can be attractive to other persons again. You will have an increased confidence level, and then things will return back to the way they are. Note, the reason for all these is just to prevent the desperation that usually follows heartbreaks.

There is another reason for doing all these.

This will help you return to that cheerful personality you used to be when your ex first met you. It will accelerate your grieve mood, and you will walk past it right away.

Getting in Contact with Your Ex

After the step of raising your confidence level, only then can you become much better and charged up to meet your ex once again. In some cases, the fact that you stop contacting them alone will raise their urge to call and want to speak with you. This is a sign that the person still cares a lot about you, but don't make the mistake of going on a date just too soon. Relax a bit and get your confidence level back on track; you should be sure you are feeling more like a happy, energetic fellow.

It doesn't matter if they never called; just ensure you have spent a couple of weeks building up your confidence, then place a call, just to say *hi*. In this call you are going to make, do not talk about the relationship, do not invite for a date, just so you know, you just placed the call to say *hi*. Do not add to that; it is very important your desperation is not seen. Let the partner know your recent activity, that you have been spending it with friends, having fun and doing something great. This is the point. It will help the partner know that you have moved past worrying about them and that is where the trick is!

But before you end the conversation, state that it will be nice if you guys did some catch up later; just don't suggest a time or place for this meeting. Just sow the thoughts in their mind and leave it there. This way, they would either return your calls or anticipate your next call.

CHAPTER SIX
DON'T AGREE ALL AT ONCE: BE HARD TO GET

Men love to chase after things that seem out of their reach. But sometimes, women tend to act wrongly with this; they would want to drive their ex into jealousy by dating someone else. This will not bring your desired result. By going into another relationship, you will expose your ex to know that the relationship you had with him was not important after all. And even if he still has feelings for you, he will not act on it.

Hence be hard to get; by this, I mean that, do not just agree to do what he suggests. Do not rush at his suggestions and calls, try to let him know that you have something doing now, and he will only be given a spare time if there are. Let his call be left unattended to and go to voicemail, and then call a few hours later. If they suggest any day to meet, try to reschedule, even if you are free at the day they had initially suggest. It is just to give them the mindset that you are not just a cheap, free person anymore (even if you used to be).

All these actions are to give him the mindset that if he wants to come into your life again, he will have to work a little bit harder. While you are at the meeting, maintain eye contacts, smile and talk freely. But place yourself on a time limit. Ensure the meeting do not just end like that; tell your ex, you have an appointment to catch with someone, but before doing this, ensure that you have given your ex some quality time. This will make them want more of your company some other time. After you leave the meeting, don't be tempted to call and ask for another date, just stay waiting it out and see if they call you first.

Have this at the back of your mind; your ex still has the reason why he breaks up with you fresh in his mind. Hence just one meeting is not enough to make the reason go away. Some more quality time is needed to renew that love, just as it were before.

But just as you play hard to get, don't cross the line to arrogance. Some ladies don't know when they finally become arrogant. They voice their strong opinions and act stubborn, sometimes; this comes along with bitterness and accusations for their partners.

They blame their ex for everything that has gone wrong in the relationship.

Don't be arrogant; it may prevent you from getting your loved one back.

Bringing back the love of your Ex

Just as explained earlier, it is very important that you don't bring up the issue with the past relationship again on your first date. After a week, place a call again after the first date. Ask about their whereabouts, their welfare; show that even in your busy schedule, you still care about them. It will mean a lot. This action can make them resolve to call you more frequently than they currently do or make them schedule another date.

If another date is scheduled, do not hesitate or play hard to get. Fall in line and agree. If you have something for that day, reschedule the other event. Try to meet as frequently as your ex wants, just after the first date. At this stage, the more you meet, the more the love you have for you improve.

Build a strong relationship

When the number of dates has increased, then you should be certain of his desires to have you back. Do not just jump into a new relationship. Take out time to check out the reason the first relationship did not work. Then analyze this so you can remove the part that will not favor this renewed love. It is now the appropriate time to talk about the past relationship, ask him in a friendly way, why he thought the past relationship did not work. Let him give you his reasons. And no matter what he says, agree with him and then mention a few reasons you have noticed too. Remember, the relationship is gone; this is not the time to point out who was right or wrong. Just agree and move on.

Check out the positive side of the relationship still, and both of you should talk about it together; the happy times, the times when you were all joyful and cheerful together. Remember the times you both saw movies together.

Don't be too Fast

The fact that you are on a date with your ex doesn't mean that you guys are back in a relationship again. Just be careful and take things slowly. Don't even ask if there is a chance for the both of you to be back again. It is too soon to ask. It will only show that you are desperate. Go out on a date, enjoy yourself.

Also, be aware that you should also focus on your personal life. Plan and improve your career. Even if getting your ex back is what you need, do not forget to climb the ladder in your career, or learn a new skill. This will help you build your confidence level. The higher your confidence, the more attractive you will be to your partner.

Don't look desperate. Take each step at a time. Good luck.

CONCLUSION

Thank you again for purchasing this book!

I hope this book was able to help you get back with your ex and build the lasting relationship you want. The next step is to go ahead and practice what you have read. Remember you have to avoid being desperate.

Finally, if you enjoyed this book, then I'd like to ask you for a favor, would you be kind enough to leave a review for this book? It'd be greatly appreciated!

Thank you and good luck!

www.ingramcontent.com/pod-product-compliance
Lightning Source LLC
Chambersburg PA
CBHW050707160426
43194CB00010B/2038